UNDERSTANDING CHATGPT FOR SCHOOL CHILDREN

DR DHEERAJ MEHROTRA

Contents

Preface

Greetings, and thank you for your interest in **"Understanding ChatGPT for School Children"** *A potent language model developed by OpenAI, ChatGPT, is the focal point of this book, intended to acquaint young learners with the captivating realm of Artificial Intelligence (AI). AI is becoming an essential component of our daily lives as we progress into the digital era, and the next generation must comprehend and utilize its capabilities.*

This book's concept was conceived to make AI accessible and enjoyable for children. AI may appear to be a complex and intimidating subject; however, this is not the case. We strive to demystify AI and demonstrate its potential as a beneficial and thrilling instrument in various life domains through interactive activities, practical examples, and engaging explanations. ChatGPT is available as your amiable guide whether you are interested in learning, creativity, problem-solving, or simply enjoying yourself.

A concerted effort has been made to ensure this book's content is educational and entertaining. Each chapter includes real-world applications, step-by-step guides, and hands-on exercises promoting active participation and exploration.

Our objective is not merely to instruct you on AI but also to motivate you to engage in critical and creative thinking regarding the potential applications of this technology in your personal life.

As you begin this voyage, you will understand how ChatGPT can assist you in your personal development, hobbies, and academic pursuits. With the aid of AI, you will acquire the ability to generate narratives, resolve issues, investigate novel topics, and establish connections with individuals worldwide. We also cover critical subjects, including the future of AI, ethical considerations, and digital safety, to guarantee that you are adequately equipped to navigate the digital landscape responsibly.

We think that each infant possesses the capacity to become a future innovator. By comprehending and adopting AI, you are initiating the process of participating in the thrilling technological developments of the future. This book is not merely a manual but an invitation to engage in exploration, learning, and creation with ChatGPT as your companion.

We are grateful to the educators, parents, and AI experts who have assisted in developing this book. Your feedback and insights have made it a comprehensive and engaging resource for young learners.

We hope this book is as thrilling to read as it was to write for all the children about to enter the world of ChatGPT. It is important to remember that learning is an endless endeavour, and with ChatGPT by your side, the possibilities are limitless. Therefore, prepare to embark on an adventure through the extraordinary potential of AI and enjoy the experience!

Wishing you a joyous reading and learning experience!

Dr Dheeraj Mehrotra

ONE

WHAT IS CHATGPT?

The Basics of ChatGPT

Hello kids! Imagine having a super-smart robot friend who can talk to you, answer your questions, and tell you stories. That's what ChatGPT is! ChatGPT is an artificial intelligence (AI) computer program that can understand and talk to people like we do. It's been trained by reading many books, websites, and other texts to learn how to converse.

ChatGPT is an AI-powered chatbot created by OpenAI. It is a significant language model capable of comprehending and producing human-like responses to diverse questions and themes. Its moniker, "Chat - GPT," refers to the "Generative Pre-trained Transformer" architecture used to train the model.

Some probable advantages of utilizing a mind map to organize information about ChatGPT:

Improved Understanding: Mind mapping can help users organize the various components of ChatGPT's capabilities, features, and limits, allowing them to communicate better with the AI model.

Efficient Navigation: A mind map can provide an overview of the various themes, subtopics, and categories associated with ChatGPT, making it easier to explore and find specific information.

Creative Exploration: Mind mapping can assist users in exploring various ChatGPT use cases, scenarios, and applications, inspiring new ideas and insights.

Collaborative Planning: A mind map can be an effective tool for collaborative planning and brainstorming among various stakeholders, including developers, academics, and ChatGPT users.

Personalized Learning: A mind map can be tailored to individual users' interests, preferences, and needs, allowing them to focus on the themes and elements of ChatGPT that are most important to them.

Employing a mind map to organize ChatGPT-related information can help users better comprehend, navigate, and explore the AI language model's possibilities.

How ChatGPT Learns

ChatGPT learns by looking at patterns in the text it reads. It's like learning new words and ideas by reading books and listening to teachers and parents. The more it reads, the better it understands and answers questions.

Why ChatGPT is Special

What makes ChatGPT unique is its ability to understand many different topics and help people with various questions. Whether you need help with your homework, want to hear a *funny joke, or need advice on a game, ChatGPT can help!*

Students have widely used ChatGPT for various academic purposes, but its success in satisfying student queries is a complex and evolving topic.

Here's a brief overview:

Information access: ChatGPT provides quick answers to many factual questions, which can be helpful for students seeking basic information.

Explanations: It can offer explanations on various topics, potentially helping students understand complex concepts.

Writing assistance: Many students use it to brainstorm ideas, outline essays, or get suggestions.

Problem-solving: It can guide students through step-by-step solutions to math or science problems.

Language learning: ChatGPT can assist with translations and language practice.

However, there are significant limitations to consider:

Accuracy: ChatGPT can sometimes provide incorrect or outdated information.

Lack of critical thinking: Over-reliance on AI might hinder students' analytical skills development.

Academic integrity: There are concerns about plagiarism and cheating when students use AI for assignments.

Depth of knowledge: While ChatGPT can provide surface-level information, it may not offer the depth required for advanced academic work.

Inability to understand context: It may not fully grasp the nuances of specific course requirements or instructor expectations.

The success of ChatGPT in satisfying student queries ultimately depends on how it's used and the specific needs of each student. While it can be a helpful tool, it's generally seen as a supplement to, rather than a replacement for, traditional learning methods and human instruction.

- *ChatGPT is like a super-smart computer friend you can talk to.*

- *You can ask it questions about almost anything, and it will try to answer.*

- *It's excellent at helping with homework or explaining tricky topics.*

- *You can use it to develop fun story ideas or play word games.*

- *ChatGPT can help you learn new things, like facts about animals or space.*

- *It's good at giving step-by-step instructions for how to do things.*

- You can ask it to explain jokes or riddles you don't understand.

- ChatGPT can help you practice writing by giving you feedback.

- It's not a natural person, so it doesn't have feelings or personal experiences.

- While it knows a lot, it can sometimes make mistakes, so always check important information with a grown-up or in a book.

- ChatGPT is a helpful tool, but it's not a substitute for learning from your teachers or parents!

TWO

How Does ChatGPT Work?

Inside ChatGPT's Brain

ChatGPT's "brain" comprises a neural network, a complex system that mimics human brains. When you ask ChatGPT a question, it uses this neural network to provide the best answer it can.

The Training Process

ChatGPT was trained using machine learning. This process involved feeding it lots of text data and teaching it to recognize patterns. Over time, it became better at understanding language and providing valuable responses.

How ChatGPT Understands Questions

When you ask ChatGPT a question, it breaks down your sentence into smaller parts and looks for keywords. It then searches its vast knowledge to find the best answer. It's like having a massive library in its brain that it can search through in seconds!

Learning about ChatGPT in steps:

- Imagine ChatGPT as a super-smart robot brain.

-

This robot brain was trained by reading millions of books and websites.

It learned patterns in how people use words and sentences.

ChatGPT reads a question or message carefully when you type it.

It thinks about all the words you used and what they mean together.

Then, it searches its "memory" for similar patterns it has seen before.

It picks out the most relevant information related to your message.

ChatGPT starts to form a response based on what it thinks you're asking.

It chooses words and phrases that make sense together.

As it builds the response, it checks if the sentences flow well.

- *It tries to make sure the answer is on-topic and helpful.*

- *ChatGPT also tries to be polite and friendly in its response.*

- *If your question was unclear, it might ask for more information.*

- *It can remember previous messages in your conversation to keep context.*

- *ChatGPT doesn't understand or feel emotions like humans do.*

- *It's just very good at putting words together in a sense-making way.*

- *Sometimes, it might make mistakes or say things that aren't true.*

-

That's why it's vital to double-check important information.

-

ChatGPT learns general patterns, but it doesn't learn from your specific conversations.

-

Whenever you chat, it's like starting fresh with its original training.

-

ChatGPT is a tool to help and inspire, but it's not a replacement for real learning or human interaction!

THREE

Fun Ways to Use ChatGPT

Learning New Things

ChatGPT *can help you learn about almost anything! If you're curious about space, dinosaurs, or how rainbows are made, ask ChatGPT, and it will answer.*

Help with Homework

Are you stuck on a math problem or need help writing a story for school? ChatGPT can provide explanations, ideas, and tips for completing your homework.

Creative Writing

ChatGPT loves to tell stories and can help you create exciting new tales. Whether you want to write a mystery, a fantasy adventure, or a funny story, ChatGPT can be your co-author.

Games and Jokes

Want to hear a joke or play a word game? ChatGPT can entertain you with fun activities and keep you laughing with its jokes.

1.
   Story writing prompts

2.
   Riddle creation and solving

3.

Language learning games

4.

Math problem generation

5.

Science experiment ideas

6.

Virtual scavenger hunts

7.

Joke telling and creation

8.

Historical figure role-playing

9.

Vocabulary builders

10.

Creative writing challenges

11.

Trivia quiz generation

12.

DIY craft instructions

13.

Simple coding tutorials

14.

Imaginative world-building

15.

Rhyme and poem creation

16.

Brainstorming for school projects

17.

"Would you rather" questions

18.

Recipe suggestions for kids' cooking

19.

Fictional character conversations

20.

Memory and word association games

21.

Time capsule idea generator

22.

"Finish the story" prompts

23.

Virtual pet care advice

24.

Inspirational quotes for kids

25.

Tongue twister creation

FOUR

Staying Safe and Smart with ChatGPT

Be Polite and Clear

When talking to ChatGPT, it's essential to be polite and straightforward. Being respectful, for example, when you talk to your friends, helps ChatGPT understand you better and provide helpful answers.

Checking Information

Sometimes, it's a good idea to double-check the information ChatGPT gives you, especially for school projects. Use other sources like books or ask your teachers to ensure everything is correct.

Privacy Matters

Remember to keep your personal information private. Don't share your full name, address, or other personal details with ChatGPT or any online tool.

Talk to Adults

Talk to an adult if you're unsure about something ChatGPT says or encounter anything that makes you uncomfortable. They can help you understand and ensure you're safe.

1.

   Use with adult supervision.

2.

Never share personal information

3.

Understand AI limitations

4.

Verify information from reliable sources

5.

Set time limits for usage

6.

Use critical thinking skills

7.

Avoid sensitive topics

8.

Report inappropriate responses

9.

Learn to spot AI-generated content

10.

Use child-friendly AI platforms when available

11.

Understand privacy policies

12.

Don't rely solely on AI for essential decisions

13.

Practice digital literacy

14.

Be aware of potential biases in AI responses

15.

Use AI as a tool, not a replacement for human interaction

16.

Discuss AI ethics with parents or teachers

17.

Learn about AI's potential and limitations

18.

Don't believe everything AI tells you

19.

Use AI to supplement, not replace, learning

20.

Be cautious about AI-generated advice

21.

Understand that AI doesn't have genuine feelings or experiences

22.

Don't use AI for homework without the teacher's approval

23.

Be aware of the potential for misinformation

24.

Learn to phrase questions effectively

25.

Understand that AI responses can be inconsistent

FIVE

The Future of ChatGPT

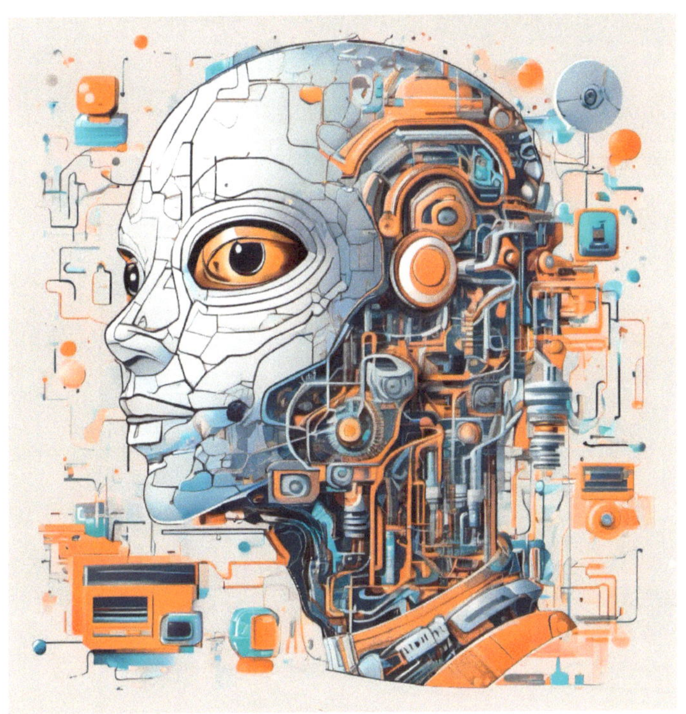

How ChatGPT is Growing

ChatGPT is constantly learning and getting better. As more people use it and provide feedback, it improves understanding and responses.

New Features and Updates

Developers are constantly developing new features and updates for ChatGPT, which means it will continue getting more innovative and helpful over time.

Imagine the Possibilities

Imagine a future where ChatGPT can help you learn new languages, explore virtual worlds, or even create video games. The possibilities are endless, and ChatGPT will help you along the way.

1.
    Enhanced natural language processing

2.
    Improved context understanding

3.
    Multilingual capabilities expansion

4.
    Integration with virtual and augmented reality

5.

Personalized learning assistance

6.

Advanced emotional intelligence

7.

Real-time information updates

8.

Seamless integration with IoT devices

9.

More accurate fact-checking abilities

10.

Customizable AI personalities

11.

Improved multimodal interactions (text, voice, image)

12.

Enhanced creative collaboration tools

13.

Specialized versions for different industries

14.

Better understanding of nuance and subtext

15.

Increased transparency in AI decision-making

16.

Integration with brain-computer interfaces

17.

Advanced problem-solving capabilities

18.

Improved long-term memory and consistency

19.

Enhanced privacy and security features

20.

Ethical AI development and implementation

SIX

ChatGPT - Your Smart Friend

ChatGPT is a fantastic tool that can help you learn, play, and explore the world in new ways. You can make the most of this incredible technology by understanding how it works and using it responsibly. So start chatting with ChatGPT, and see where your curiosity takes you!

ChatGPT is a remarkable tool that has opened up new possibilities for learning, creativity, and problem-solving. This artificial intelligence language model, developed by OpenAI, has captured the imagination of millions worldwide with its ability to engage in human-like conversations across a vast range of topics.

One of ChatGPT's greatest strengths is its versatility as a learning aid. It can explain complex concepts in simple terms, provide summaries of difficult subjects, and offer step-by-step guidance on problem-solving. This makes it an invaluable resource for students struggling with challenging topics or anyone looking to expand their knowledge in new areas. From history to science, literature to mathematics, ChatGPT can serve as a patient tutor, always ready to elaborate or rephrase explanations until the user grasps the concept.

Beyond academics, ChatGPT shines as a creative companion. Writers can use it to brainstorm ideas, overcome writer's block, or get feedback. Artists might engage with it to explore new perspectives or generate unique concepts. ChatGPT can offer fresh insights and inspire innovative approaches even in fields like music or game design.

For professionals and hobbyists alike, ChatGPT can be a powerful tool for problem-solving and creativity. It can help break down complex issues, suggest alternative viewpoints, or provide quick access to general information that can spark new solutions. Whether you're a software developer debugging code, a business strategist planning a new initiative, or a DIY enthusiast tackling a home project, ChatGPT can offer valuable suggestions and insights.

However, to truly harness ChatGPT's potential, it's crucial to understand its limitations and use it responsibly. While impressively knowledgeable, ChatGPT can sometimes provide inaccurate information or biased viewpoints. It's trained on data with a cutoff date, meaning its knowledge of current events is limited. Users should always verify essential details from authoritative sources and approach ChatGPT's outputs critically.

Ethical use of ChatGPT is paramount, especially in academic and professional settings. It should enhance learning and productivity, not as a shortcut to avoid developing crucial skills. Plagiarism and misrepresenting AI-generated content as one's work are severe concerns that users must actively avoid.

Moreover, users should be mindful of privacy considerations when interacting with ChatGPT. Avoid sharing sensitive personal information or confidential data during conversations.

Despite these caveats, ChatGPT's potential to enrich our lives is immense. It can serve as a language learning partner, helping users practice conversations in foreign languages. It can act as a sounding board for personal reflections or ethical dilemmas, offering different perspectives. For those with limited access to human experts, ChatGPT can provide a level of guidance and information that was previously unavailable.

As we continue exploring ChatGPT's capabilities, we will discover even more innovative applications. The key is approaching it with curiosity, creativity, and critical thinking. Use it to supplement and enhance your knowledge and skills, not to replace them.

In conclusion, ChatGPT represents a significant leap forward in AI technology, offering a uniquely accessible and versatile tool for learning, creativity, and problem-solving. By understanding its strengths and limitations, using it responsibly, and combining its capabilities with our critical thinking, we can leverage ChatGPT to expand our horizons, boost our productivity, and explore new realms of possibility. The future of human-AI interaction is here, and ChatGPT is just the beginning. So dive in, explore, and let your curiosity guide you through this fascinating new landscape of knowledge and creativity.

SEVEN

42

ChatGPT in Everyday Life

ChatGPT as a Study Buddy

Imagine having a study buddy ready to help you anytime and anywhere. That's what ChatGPT can be! Whether studying for a test or learning something new, ChatGPT can explain concepts, quiz you, and even help you memorize facts.

ChatGPT for Hobbies

Do you have a hobby like drawing, coding, or playing an instrument? ChatGPT can provide tips, tutorials, and inspiration. It can also help you find new projects to work on and answer questions about your hobby.

ChatGPT for Family Fun

ChatGPT can also be a fun tool for the whole family. You can use it to plan family activities, find recipes for cooking together, or even play trivia games during family nights.

1.
   Personal assistant for scheduling and reminders

2.
   Recipe suggestions and meal planning

3.
   Quick language translation

4.
   Homework helper and study aid

5.

Mental health support and mood tracking

6.

Financial advice and budgeting assistance

7.

Travel planning and local recommendations

8.

News summarization and analysis

9.

Home automation control

10.

Fitness and workout planning

11.

Creative writing partner

12.

DIY project guidance

13.

Career advice and resume-building

14.

Technical troubleshooting

15.

Personalized   entertainment recommendations

16.

Social media content creation

17.

Fact-checking and research aid

18.

Personal growth and self-improvement coach

19.

Quick medical symptom assessment (non-emergency)

20.

Environmental impact tracking for daily choices

EIGHT

• 48 •

CREATING WITH CHATGPT

Writing Stories Together

One of the most fun things you can do with ChatGPT is to write stories. Start with an idea, and ChatGPT will help you build the story, create characters, and add exciting twists and turns.

Writing stories with ChatGPT provides an experience that is both interactive and dynamic, enabling you to go deeply into the realm of fiction to create your narrative. To make the procedure even more fun, here are some methods that we can use:

Creation of Characters: We can create complex and diverse characters, each with its history, personalities, and reasons for doing what it does. Are you looking for a courageous protagonist or a crafty antagonist? Together, let's devise them, shall we?

World-building involves creating intricate settings that immerse you in the novel's world. These settings might range from enchanted forests to futuristic cities. Describe the universe you envision for yourself, and we will construct it step by step.

The plot development: Whether you want a slow-burning mystery or an action-packed adventure, we can sketch the plot, generate suspense, and organize important events. We will ensure that each chapter maintains the readers' interest.

Dialogue and Interaction: Creating realistic and exciting dialogue can help bring your characters to life. We can compose discussions that illustrate their personalities and propel the narrative forward.

It is vital to incorporate unexpected components to maintain the story's unpredictable and exciting nature. Surprises that put your characters to the test and excite your audience are something we can come up with together.

Infuse your narrative with deeper meanings and ideas by incorporating them. Whether it's a story about friendship, adventure, or redemption, we can weave messages that resonate with the audience.

Collaborative editing allows you to improve and perfect your tale. We can evaluate and alter scenes, ensuring consistency and enhancing the work's quality.

Are you ready to embark on your adventure of storytelling? Give me your idea, and together, we can create a story to captivate your audience!

Making Art with ChatGPT

You can also use ChatGPT to generate creative ideas for your art projects. Whether you're painting, drawing, or crafting, ChatGPT can suggest themes, colours, and techniques to try.

ChatGPT is a flexible tool that has the potential to stimulate your creative process and provide inspiration for your artistic endeavours. Whether you express yourself artistically through painting, drawing, crafts, or any other medium, ChatGPT can offer new ideas and suggestions to help you improve your work. If you are looking for a topic, for example, ChatGPT can assist you in coming up with ideas such as "urban fantasy," "nature's contrasts," or "abstract emotions."

When it comes to colour schemes, ChatGPT can provide harmonious or dramatic colour combinations that clash to make your artwork stand out. Imagine experimenting with a colour scheme reminiscent of a winter landscape, with chilly tones and brilliant oranges, purples, and pinks, or a palette inspired by a sunset, with vibrant oranges, purples, and pinks.

Moreover, ChatGPT can present you with novel approaches and methodologies. Are you interested in experimenting with pointillism, combining watercolour, or mixed-media collage? ChatGPT can offer instruction and advice in a step-by-step format to help users grasp these strategies. It may also recommend combining texture, light, and shadow into your creations to provide depth and dimension.

Not only can ChatGPT provide you with technical guidance, but it can also provide you with inspirational quotes, extracts from art history, or even fictional backstories for your pieces, which can enrich your creative process. Let ChatGPT serve as your virtual muse, leading you through your artistic journey and assisting you in bringing your idea to life. Embrace the boundless possibilities that are available to you.

Building Projects

If you enjoy building things with LEGO, coding robots, or doing science projects, ChatGPT can be your guide. It can provide instructions, troubleshoot problems, and suggest new ideas to relax your projects.

LEGO Construction: ChatGPT can suggest imaginative LEGO creations based on your hobbies, such as architectural marvels, cars, or fantasy worlds. This service is directed toward LEGO aficionados. ChatGPT can advise on structural stability, colour schemes, and intricate detailing if you cannot move on with a challenging design. In addition, it can suggest several methods to personalize your builds, ensuring each project is unique to you.

Coding Robots: If you are interested in robotics, ChatGPT can help you learn how to use a variety of programming languages, such as

Python, Scratch, or C++. Whether you are constructing a straightforward line-following robot or a complicated humanoid, ChatGPT can give you detailed directions on how to code, assist you in debugging your code, and make suggestions for enhancements. This can also allow you to learn about new robotics platforms and challenges, which will help you improve your skills and keep your projects interesting.

For science projects, ChatGPT can be a veritable treasury of ideas and information for those who are passionate about science. It can suggest experiments in physics, chemistry, biology, or environmental science, complete with thorough protocols and explanations of the scientific ideas that underlie the experiments. If you run into problems, ChatGPT can assist you in troubleshooting experimental setups, interpreting data, and suggesting potential improvements to improve your investigations.

In addition to providing instructions and assisting with troubleshooting, ChatGPT may also help ignite your creative side. It can recommend interdisciplinary projects that mix LEGO, robotics, and science. For example, it could suggest constructing a robotic arm out of LEGO and programming it to carry out particular tasks. Alternatively, tests that incorporate technology and engineering principles could be offered.

ChatGPT can recommend books, online courses, and tutorials that can help you gain a deeper understanding of your hobbies on a personal level. Additionally, it can connect you with online groups and forums where you may discuss your creations, receive feedback, and collaborate with others with similar interests.

Planning the Project ChatGPT can assist with planning and organization for more substantial projects. It can help you break down tasks, establish timelines, and properly manage resources, which will ensure that your projects are completed smoothly and efficiently.

ChatGPT is a versatile companion that can provide support, inspiration, and expertise, making your creative path more pleasurable and gratifying. Whether you are exploring new hobbies or want to enhance the ones you already have, ChatGPT can help.

NINE

25 Tips For Managing ChatGPT Effectively

25 tips for using ChatGPT effectively:

1.

Be specific in your queries to get more accurate responses.

2.

Use follow-up questions to dive deeper into a topic.

3.

Experiment with different phrasings if you're not satisfied with an initial response.

4.

Provide context when asking complex questions.

5.

Break down large tasks into more minor, manageable queries.

6.

Use ChatGPT to brainstorm ideas and overcome creative blocks.

7.

Ask for explanations of concepts you don't understand.

8.

Request step-by-step guides for complex processes.

9.

Use it to practice foreign languages through conversation.

10.

Ask for pros and cons when making decisions.

11.

Utilize it for proofreading and grammar checks.

12.

Request summaries of long texts or complex ideas.

13.

Use it to generate outlines for essays or articles.

14.

Ask for analogies to help understand complex concepts.

15.

Use it to explore different perspectives on a topic.

16.

Request examples to illustrate abstract ideas.

17.

Use it for quick fact-checking, but verify critical information.

18.

Ask for tips on improving specific skills.

19.

Use it to break down complex problems into smaller parts.

20.

Request formatting help for various types of documents.

21.

Use it to generate practice questions for study sessions.

22.

Ask for explanations of industry-specific jargon.

23.

Use it to explore hypothetical scenarios.

24.

Request time management and productivity tips.

25.

Remember to critically evaluate all responses and use them as a starting point rather than definitive answers.

TEN

Fun Activities with ChatGPT

Here are the top 50 fun activities you can do with ChatGPT:

1.

    Play word games like 20 Questions or I Spy

2.

    Engage in creative writing exercises

3.

Create and solve riddles

4.

Brainstorm ideas for a short story or novel

5.

Have a mock debate on a silly topic

6.

Generate writing prompts and respond to them

7.

Create fictional character backstories

8.

Play a text-based role-playing game

9.

Invent new recipes for imaginary dishes

10.

Compose silly poems or limericks

11.

Create alternate history scenarios

12.

Design a fictional world or universe

13.

Generate and solve math puzzles

14.

Play a game of "Would You Rather"

15.

Create punny jokes

16.

Develop a fictional language

17.

Write dialogue for imaginary movie scenes

18.

Create bizarre superhero origin stories

19.

Invent new sports or games with rules

20.

Generate ideas for wacky inventions

21.

Create a bucket list for a fictional character

22.

Play a text-based adventure game

23.

Write song lyrics in different genres

24.

Create tongue twisters

25.

Design escape room puzzles

26.

Develop a fictional company with products

27.

Create "What If" scenarios and explore outcomes

28.

Write horoscopes for made-up zodiac signs

29.

Invent new holidays with traditions

30.

Create a fictional travel guide for an imaginary place

31.

Write fortune cookie messages

32.

Develop backstories for inanimate objects

33.

Create nonsensical scientific theories

34.

Write headlines for a tabloid newspaper

35.

Invent new phobias and their descriptions

36.

Create a menu for a themed restaurant

37.

Write motivational speeches for unlikely scenarios

38.

Develop a fictional conspiracy theory

39.

Create a list of rules for an imaginary society

40.

Write diary entries for historical figures in modern times

41.

Invent new genres of music and describe them

42.

Create a fictional self-help book title and chapter list

43.

Write product descriptions for impossible items

44.

Develop a dating profile for a mythical creature

45.

Create a schedule for a bizarre theme park

46.

Write instructions for everyday tasks as if for aliens

47.

Invent new categories for award shows

48.

Create job descriptions for fictional careers

49.

Write a manifesto for a silly cause

50.

Develop a workout routine using household items.

These activities can provide hours of entertainment and creativity. Remember, the key is to let your imagination run wild and have fun with the limitless possibilities ChatGPT offers.

ELEVEN

CHATGPT FOR PARENTS AND TEACHERS

Here are 25 ways parents and teachers can use ChatGPT:

1.

    Generate age-appropriate lesson plans

2.

    Create customized homework assignments

3.

Develop interactive storytelling exercises

4.

Provide explanations for complex topics in simple terms

5.

Generate quiz questions for test preparation

6.

Offer suggestions for engaging in classroom activities

7.

Help create individualized learning plans for students

8.

Provide ideas for educational games and puzzles

9.

Assist in writing report card comments

10.

Generate creative writing prompts for students

11.

Offer strategies for managing classroom behaviour

12.

Provide tips for effective parent-teacher communication

13.

Help create visual aids and infographics for lessons

14.

Suggest methods for teaching complex concepts

15.

Offer advice on inclusive education practices

16.

Help design project-based learning activities

17.

Provide ideas for science fair projects

18.

Assist in creating rubrics for assignments

19.

Offer suggestions for educational field trips

20.

Help develop strategies for students with special needs

21.

Provide ideas for engaging reluctant learners

22.

Assist in creating study guides for various subjects

23.

Offer tips for promoting reading habits in children

24.

Help design differentiated instruction strategies

25.

Provide suggestions for incorporating technology in the classroom

These applications can be tailored to specific grade levels, subjects, or student needs.

TWELVE

Fun Experiments with ChatGPT

Here are the top 30 fun experiments with ChatGPT for kids:

1.

    Create a silly story by taking turns adding sentences

2.

Invent a new animal and describe its habitat and behaviours

3.

Design a treasure hunt with clues and riddles

4.

Create a comic strip dialogue

5.

Invent nonsense words and define them

6.

Play "Guess the Animal" with yes/no questions

7.

Write a recipe for a magical potion

8.

Please create a new planet and describe its features

9.

Design a board game with unique rules

10.

Write a short play with funny characters

11.

Invent a new holiday and its traditions

12.

Create a secret code language

13.

Design a treehouse with impossible features

14.

Invent a new flavour of ice cream and describe it

15.

Create a superhero and their origin story

16.

Write lyrics for a silly song

17.

Design a maze with interesting obstacles

18.

Invent a new sport and explain its rules

19.

Create a "Day in the Life" story for a household object

20.

Design a time machine and describe how it works

21.

Invent new names for colours and describe them

22.

Create a "Mad Libs" style story

23.

Design a robot helper and list its functions

24.

Invent a new type of transportation

25.

Create a "What If" scenario (e.g., "What if cats could talk?")

26.

Design a crazy obstacle course

27.

Invent a new type of candy and describe its effects

28.

Create a backstory for a constellation

29.

Design a theme park based on a book or movie

30.

Invent a new school subject and describe what students would learn

These experiments can help kids develop creativity, improve language skills, and have fun while interacting with AI technology. Remember to supervise children's use of ChatGPT and encourage them to think critically about the responses they receive.

THIRTEEN

CHATGPT AND THE ENVIRONMENT

Here are 25 ways ChatGPT can be helpful for kids learning about the environment:

1.

    Eco-friendly tip generator

2.

    Recycling guides

3.

Environmental fact quizzes

4.

Climate change explanations

5.

Endangered species information

6.

Energy conservation ideas

7.

Water-saving challenges

8.

Pollution causes and effects

9.

Eco-system role-playing games

10.

Sustainable living suggestions

11.

Environmental science project ideas

12.

Green technology explanations

13.

Nature observation prompts

14.

Composting tutorials

15.

Carbon footprint calculators

16.

Environmental hero biographies

17.

Eco-friendly craft ideas

18.

Plant identification assistance

19.

Weather pattern discussions

20.

Renewable energy explanations

21.

Ocean conservation facts

22.

Environmental policy simplifications

23.

Eco-vocabulary builders

24.

Environmental debate topics

25.

Green career exploration

FOURTEEN

WORKING ON CHATGPT - A SAMPLE SCREEN SHARE

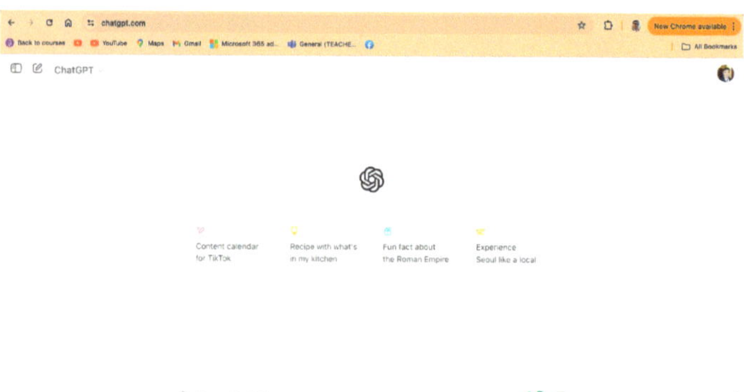

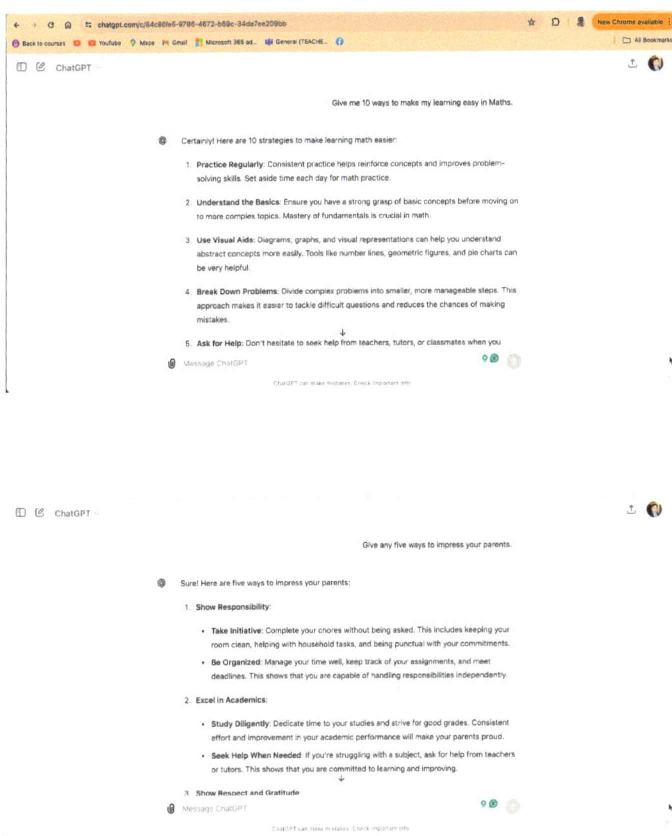

Give me 10 ways to make my learning easy in Maths.

Certainly! Here are 10 strategies to make learning math easier:

1. Practice Regularly: Consistent practice helps reinforce concepts and improves problem-solving skills. Set aside time each day for math practice.

2. Understand the Basics: Ensure you have a strong grasp of basic concepts before moving on to more complex topics. Mastery of fundamentals is crucial in math.

3. Use Visual Aids: Diagrams, graphs, and visual representations can help you understand abstract concepts more easily. Tools like number lines, geometric figures, and pie charts can be very helpful.

4. Break Down Problems: Divide complex problems into smaller, more manageable steps. This approach makes it easier to tackle difficult questions and reduces the chances of making mistakes.

5. Ask for Help: Don't hesitate to seek help from teachers, tutors, or classmates when you

Message ChatGPT

ChatGPT can make mistakes. Check important info.

Give any five ways to impress your parents.

Sure! Here are five ways to impress your parents:

1. Show Responsibility:
   • Take Initiative: Complete your chores without being asked. This includes keeping your room clean, helping with household tasks, and being punctual with your commitments.
   • Be Organized: Manage your time well, keep track of your assignments, and meet deadlines. This shows that you are capable of handling responsibilities independently.

2. Excel in Academics:
   • Study Diligently: Dedicate time to your studies and strive for good grades. Consistent effort and improvement in your academic performance will make your parents proud.
   • Seek Help When Needed: If you're struggling with a subject, ask for help from teachers or tutors. This shows that you are committed to learning and improving.

3. Show Respect and Gratitude:

Message ChatGPT

ChatGPT can make mistakes. Check important info.

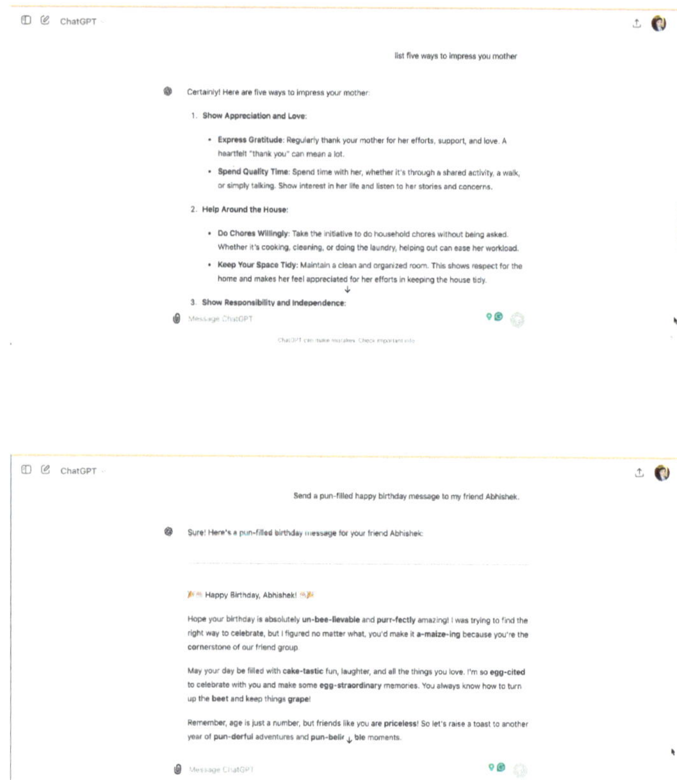
ChatGPT

list five ways to impress you mother

Certainly! Here are five ways to impress your mother:

1. Show Appreciation and Love:

• Express Gratitude: Regularly thank your mother for her efforts, support, and love. A heartfelt "thank you" can mean a lot.

• Spend Quality Time: Spend time with her, whether it's through a shared activity, a walk, or simply talking. Show interest in her life and listen to her stories and concerns.

2. Help Around the House:

• Do Chores Willingly: Take the initiative to do household chores without being asked. Whether it's cooking, cleaning, or doing the laundry, helping out can ease her workload.

• Keep Your Space Tidy: Maintain a clean and organized room. This shows respect for the home and makes her feel appreciated for her efforts in keeping the house tidy.

3. Show Responsibility and Independence:

Message ChatGPT

ChatGPT

Send a pun-filled happy birthday message to my friend Abhishek.

Sure! Here's a pun-filled birthday message for your friend Abhishek:

🎉🎈 Happy Birthday, Abhishek! 🎂🎉

Hope your birthday is absolutely un-bee-lievable and purr-fectly amazing! I was trying to find the right way to celebrate, but I figured no matter what, you'd make it a-maize-ing because you're the cornerstone of our friend group.

May your day be filled with cake-tastic fun, laughter, and all the things you love. I'm so egg-cited to celebrate with you and make some egg-straordinary memories. You always know how to turn up the beet and keep things grape!

Remember, age is just a number, but friends like you are priceless! So let's raise a toast to another year of pun-derful adventures and pun-believable moments.

Message ChatGPT

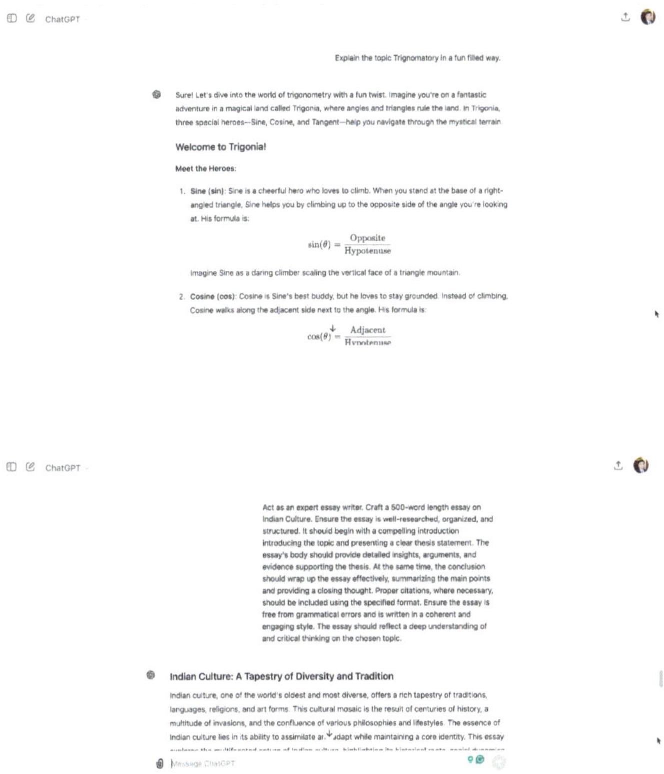

Some Important Prompts for Students:

1. What are some key terms I should know about [topic]?
2. What are some important concepts in [subject]?
3. Provide me with some reliable sources to learn about [topic].
4. I want you to act as a research assistant and provide me with 5 reliable sources to learn about [topic].

1. What does [term] mean?
2. Can you explain [concept] to me?
3. Define [term] and provide an example.
4. Can you explain the concept of [topic] in simple terms?
5. What is the difference between [term1] and [term2]?
6. Craft a sentence using [word] in context.
7. I want you to act as a teacher and give me a definition of [term].

1. What are some best practices for [topic]
2. What are the advantages and disadvantages of [concept]?
3. What are the benefits of [concept]?
4. Can you give me some examples of [topic] in real life?
5. What are some common mistakes to avoid when [activity]?
6. Suggest some strategies for improving [skill].
7. I want you to act as an [subject] expert and give me recommendations for [specific question].

1. Describe the main points of [book] in a few sentences.
2. Craft a brief summary of [topic].
3. Can you provide an overview of [concept] and its significance?
4. Generate a bullet-point list of key takeaways from [presentation].
5. Summarize in a few short sentences: [sentence]
6. Explain this for 5 years old: [sentence]

1. Give me step-by-step instructions on how to learn [skill].
2. Explain the basics of [subject] for beginners.
3. Can you provide me with some exercises to practice [skill]?

1. Give me some book recommendations on [topic].
2. Can you recommend some blogs to follow for [topic]?
3. Generate a list of books on [subject].
4. Suggest me 3 apps for learning [French]

1. List some related topics to [subject] that I should explore.
2. Can you suggest some resources for learning more about [topic]?
3. Describe the relationship between [concept1] and [concept2].
4. Explain how [subject] relates to [field].
5. List some other approaches to [topic] that I could explore.

1. Create a quiz on [topic] with 10 questions.
2. Generate a fill-in-the-blank exercise on [concept].
3. Come up with a multiple-choice exercise to test knowledge of [skill].

1. Describe some effective study strategies for [subject].
2. Give me some tips on how to stay motivated while learning [topic].
3. Explain how to manage time effectively when studying [subject].
4. Provide some advice for staying organized while learning [topic].

Books By The Same Author

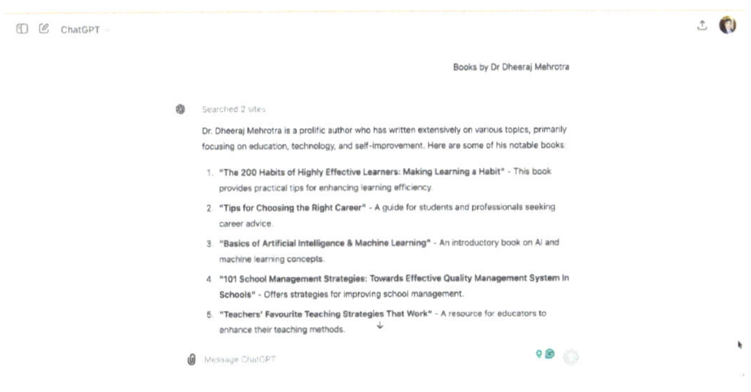

Do Visit

www.authordheerajmehrotra.comhttps://rebrand.ly/
xlp11ra

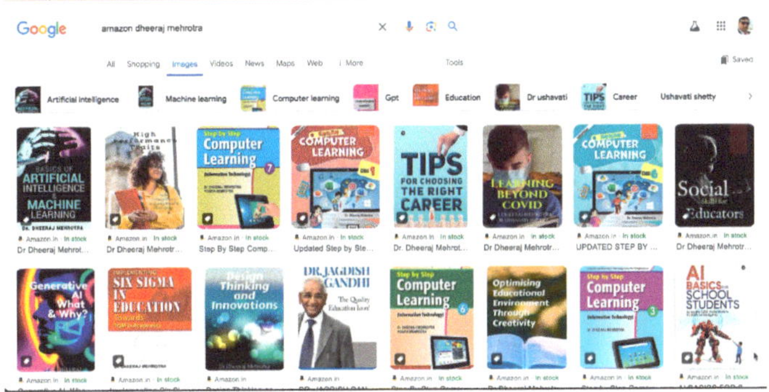

About The Author

Dheeraj Mehrotra, MS, MPhil, PhD (Education Management)., a white and a yellow belt in SIX SIGMA, a Certified NLP Business Diploma holder, is an Educational Innovator, Author, with expertise in Six Sigma In Education, Academic Audits, Neuro-Linguistic Programming (NLP), Total Quality Management In Education, an Experiential Educator, a CBSE Resource towards School Assessment (SQAA), CCE, JIT, Five S, and KAIZEN. He has authored over 100 books on computer science, AI, digital body language, NLP, quality circles, school management, classroom effectiveness, and safety and security. A former Principal at De Indian Public School, New Delhi, (INDIA), NPS International School, Guwahati, and Education Officer at GEMS, Gurgaon, with ample teaching experience of over Three Decades, he is a certified Trainer for Quality Circles/ TQM in Education and QCI Standards for School Accreditation/ School Audits and Management. He has also been honoured with the President of India's National Teacher Award in 2006 and the Best Science Teacher State Award (By the Ministry of Science and Technology, State of UP), Innovation in Education for his inception of Six Sigma In Education by Education Watch, New Delhi and Education World- Best Teacher Award, BOLT Learner Teacher Award by Air India, 'Innovation in Education Award 2016' by Higher Education Forum (HEF), Gujarat Chapter, among others. He has developed over 150 FREE EDUCATIONAL MOBILE Apps for the Google Play Store exclusively for Teachers, Students, and Parents. This work has been recognised by the LIMCA BOOK OF RECORDS and INDIA BOOK OF RECORDS as the only Indian to draw that feast. As a founder and president of the IoT Society of India, he also promotes Technology Globally. Dr Mehrotra is presently engaged as a PRINCIPAL at KUNWARS GLOBAL SCHOOL, Lucknow, India. He has conducted over 2000 workshops globally on "Excellence In Education" integrated with Total Quality Management and Six Sigma, Technology Integration in Education (TIE), Developing towards being ROCKSTAR TEACHERS, including Cyberspace, Cyber Security, Classroom Management, School Leadership & Management, and Innovative teaching within classrooms via Mind Maps, NLP and Experiential Learning in Academics. He is an active TEDx speaker and can be viewed on the YouTube TEDx channel. As a premium UDEMY Instructor, he has developed over 500 courses and caters to over 8 Lakh students from 180 countries. He can be visited at www.authordheerajmehrotra.com

www.authordheerajmehrotra.com